AMERICAN OPINION
&
THE WAR

AMERICAN OPINION

&

THE WAR

By

ARCHIBALD MacLEISH

The Librarian of Congress at Washington, D.C.

THE REDE LECTURE
DELIVERED BEFORE THE UNIVERSITY
OF CAMBRIDGE ON
30 JULY
1942

CAMBRIDGE

AT THE UNIVERSITY PRESS

1942

CAMBRIDGE
UNIVERSITY PRESS

University Printing House, Cambridge CB2 8BS, United Kingdom

Published in the United States of America by Cambridge University Press, New York

Cambridge University Press is part of the University of Cambridge.

It furthers the University's mission by disseminating knowledge in the pursuit of
education, learning and research at the highest international levels of excellence.

www.cambridge.org
Information on this title: www.cambridge.org/9781107699380

© Cambridge University Press 1942

First published 1942
Re-issued 2014

A catalogue record for this publication is available from the British Library

ISBN 978-1-107-69938-0 Paperback

AMERICAN OPINION & THE WAR

TO be invited to give the Rede Lecture is, I imagine, a disconcerting experience even for a member of a race which is notoriously difficult to disconcert. There should be no question therefore of its effect upon an American. Not only the names of one's distinguished predecessors on this platform but the platform, and the place itself, loom large across the Atlantic. There are certain doors through which a man cannot pass without measuring himself humbly against the door-post, and the doors of Oxford and of Cambridge are of this kind. The time is long past when American writers thought of themselves as provincials of the world of English letters. For better or for worse, there will never be another Henry James. But neither, I think, will the time ever come when American writers can return to the great English foundations of our common English culture without humility. English is more than a tongue: more than a literature. English is a life also, and a life we are at once proud and humble to share—not with you, the living, only, but with those also who were here before you in these famous cities.

To attempt to speak of these things as it is fitting men should speak of them is to accept a heavy burden and a responsibility no one who loves the English tongue would wish to bear. I am not altogether unhappy therefore that the times in which we live, and the particular circumstances of my visit to England, have made it impossible for me to undertake the task your invitation would have put upon me in an ordinary year. It is impossible, in the circumstances of the changing war, to think or speak of things which do not change. We feel, all of us, like messengers in a tragic play—messengers whose only endurable task is to see, and to report what we have seen. The heroes of the piece and the devoted victims will deliver, when the time arrives, the appropriate speeches, but for ourselves there is this duty only: to communicate in honesty and in simplicity the things that we have seen. 'That which I have myself seen', as Bernal Diaz put it, 'and the fighting…'.

It is this duty—for so I conceive it—I wish to perform here this afternoon. What I have seen is the reaction of my country to seven months of war. And what I wish to speak of is the state of mind and heart of my country— the thinking of my country about our common experience and the meaning of that thinking as I understand it. More precisely, what I wish to speak of is the discussion in the United States of the purpose of the war, and the two sides taken in debate upon that subject, and why these sides are taken.

You in England, I suppose, have long since passed this point in your discussions with each other. You have spoken to each other at great length and over many months of the purposes for which you mean to fight and you have come, doubtless, to your own conclusions. But you must understand that we in my country have never faced this question until now: that we have been, indeed, unable until now to face it. It is not difficult, I think, to understand the reason. Down to the time when the Japanese attacked us at Pearl Harbor, our talk of war was talk, not of affirmative purpose, but defence. Our only question was the question whether we should fight at all. The debate among us was debate upon the issue whether it was true we also were in danger—whether we too would be attacked and must prepare. That the United States should make a war affirmatively and of its own motion to accomplish some end or purpose of its own was in no one's mind. Even those who saw most clearly what fascism was, and who hated it most bitterly, and were most determined to destroy it, had nothing to say in those months of any choice or purpose we might offer to ourselves. The only choice we were called on then to make was the choice our enemies presented to us—the choice to fight while we still could—while we had friends to help us— or else to fight too late.

If there were some who saw at that time—who had seen indeed from the beginning of the fascist invasion of Spain and the Japanese invasion of China—that fascism was actually no more than a belated rear-guard gathering of the forces free men had always attacked before, and must now attack again, and that the true offensive in this war was therefore ours, they were not heard. No one of responsibility in our country nor, I think, in yours, called upon his fellow-citizens to attack the fascists first and to carry through, against the old reaction, the democratic revolution which reaction once again had challenged. The only hope, even of the most belligerent democrats, was the hope that their fellow-citizens might resist in time. We were the peaceful powers and these others were the aggressors. We were those who stood and they were those who struck. They were the attackers, we were the attacked. The attacked do not consider for what purpose they propose to fight. They consider only how and where and when they will defend themselves.

So that it was not possible for us to consider as a nation through those months the purposes for which we ought to fight. It was not possible for us to propose to ourselves the ends or objects which our military effort as a people should attain. Had any American suggested to his fellow-citizens in 1938 or 1939 or even 1940 that we of our own motion should attack the declared enemies of democracy and freedom in order to destroy them and to establish once and for all a free and decent world in which democracy could live and thrive and ripen, he would have found no listeners. We had no stomach then for the establishment of new worlds.

But all this was in no way peculiar to us. No other democratic nation would have turned to war of its own volition in those years, or attempted any alteration of the world which only violence could accomplish. With us as with you the great body of the people desired only peace and the one question in their minds was the question whether peace must be secured by fighting or could be

8

had without. With us no more than with any other democratic nation did the people will the war. Indeed, with us, the fighting of the war was even less of our election than it was with you, for even at the moment when we found ourselves at war we had not willed it. The choice was made against us by our enemies. We were attacked while still at peace and our determination to resist was fixed and hardened after our resistance had been made.

Other democratic nations so far shaped their purpose to make war as to declare their purpose when they had no choice but fight. With us the declaration followed on a war already made. Certain determinations there had been—determinations requiring the great courage of a great leader—the determination to make our factories and goods available to those who had already been attacked and were resisting—the determination to assist by every method short of war those who like ourselves believed in human decency and freedom—the determination to take action for our own defence in spite of threats abroad and menaces at home. But though our position was clear both to our friends and to our enemies, it was not we, at the final moment, who determined on our action, nor did we consider then or for many months thereafter where our action ought to lead.

Our first response to the attack upon us was the natural response of angry and indignant men. I may be excused perhaps for saying that it was the response of men of courage also. In the face of a considerable defeatist propaganda in sections of the press and the open demand of at least one politician that the fleet should be returned for the defence of their own shores, the American people were almost unanimous in their demand for an offensive war— a war carried to their enemies. They are still unanimous in that opinion. But though the temper of the country changed from defensive to offensive within a few days— perhaps even within a few hours—of the attack on Pearl Harbor, the attitude of the country toward the war itself did not change. It was still the enemy's war—the fascist's war—a war made *by* them *upon* us. We were determined to win that war. We were determined to chastise those who had made the war against us: to defeat them so effectively and so finally that they would regret what they had done to the end of their history—if any history were left them. We were determined in short to turn their war against its authors. But we were not yet ready to take it for ourselves—to turn it into an instrument of our own purpose for the accomplishment of our own ends as freedom-loving men and women.

It was understandable I think—understandable in terms of your own experience in your country as well as ours in ours—that we were not ready. For one thing the mere shock of the actual encounter itself engrossed us at the beginning: there was too much to be done too quickly to give us time for anything but what lay just ahead. For another, we had our new-found unity to think of. On December 7th we were all of one mind about the war and so long as the war remained a war against the Japanese who had tricked us and the Nazis who had set them to it—so long as it was merely a war *against* our enemies and not a war for some positive purpose of our own—we would continue to think of it with one mind. All men will agree upon resistance to a common danger, but all men will not agree—and it is the tragedy of human history that they will not—upon the winning of a common hope. Unity, in the months immediately following Pearl Harbor, seemed to most Americans the most important thing the country could attain. The divisions of the year before had been acrimonious and bitter, and though they were for the most part personal divisions—divisions created by a handful of men and women who put their personal animosity to the President above their duty to their country—everyone in every party wished to see them healed. There was therefore a truce of several months' duration to all discussions of the causes and the meaning of the war—a truce adopted by common consent and resting upon a common appreciation of the seriousness of the country's situation. Those who had foreseen the inevitability of American resistance held their tongues, and those who had believed and said that the war was a European war which need never touch the American people accepted the final verdict of events.

That this undeclared truce served a useful and creative purpose most Americans will, I think, admit. Those who had not agreed before, and could scarcely be expected to agree explicitly now, were able to meet each other in a common necessity for action, and the greater part of the pre-war minority were joined again with the vast majority of the people who had supported the President's policy long before history had made the wisdom of his policy irrefutably clear. But though the truce upon discussion of the meaning and the purpose of the war served useful ends, it had also its increasingly apparent disadvantages. It silenced questions which could not be silenced. Not the partisans of the old dispute but people everywhere throughout the country were beginning to think what no one wished to say. For what actually were we fighting? Were we fighting a war to accomplish something or only a war to prevent something? Were we fighting a war to prevent defeat or a war to accomplish victory; and if the latter, what kind of victory? What would the world be like when the war ended? Would it be a world like the world at the end of the last war or a different world and, if so, in what way different and how did we propose to bring about the difference? The questions asked themselves and were not answered. And gradually, as the pressure of the asking grew, men in the government like men outside it came to understand that unity of the nation could only be secured not by silencing these questions but by answering them—that they must be answered—that the people had a right to have them answered.

It is this that constitutes the change in American opinion of which I wish to speak to you. The visible evidence of change is the response of leaders of the American government to the questioning and searching of the people. It is evidence which has come, I think, to your notice in this country. Over the course of the last few weeks a number of members of the government in Washington have spoken, as though with one mind and by preconceived plan, of the purposes for which the war is fought. Not only the Vice-President but our Ambassador here and the Under-Secretary of State, Mr Welles, and the Assistant Secretary, Mr Acheson, and Mr Milo Perkins of the Board of Economic Warfare, have spoken in one way or another of the world we mean to establish when the war is done— the world we, with our allies of the democratic powers, mean to build—the century, as Mr Wallace puts it, of the common man. These speeches moreover have not only been given: they have been received. They have been read and listened to and discussed. And they have been discussed for the most part with an enthusiasm and an excitement which is quite astonishing.

That the American people have expressed, in their reaction to these speeches and in other ways, an altered and a far more positive attitude toward the war, seems to me unarguable. It is difficult to measure popular opinion in any quantitative sense. Certainly the so-called 'opinion polls' now employed on both sides of the Atlantic are not instruments of precision, nor is the space given by the press to the discussion of any particular issue an infallible measure of the public interest. Newspaper publishers have been known in our country—I cannot speak of course for yours—to consult their private preferences in arriving at their estimates of public interest, and even, it is said, to attempt to excite a public interest where no interest had previously been shown—or else to starve with silence an interest they deplore. Nevertheless both press coverage and opinion polls are indicative to some extent, and in so far as they are indicative their testimony is all to one effect. Mr Wallace's Free World Dinner speech, ignored at first by the greater part of the press, was belatedly driven into the columns of the principal papers by the sheer weight of private concern—an unusual phenomenon in any country —and Mr Sumner Welles's speech on the same subject was reported promptly in an unusually emphatic manner. As for the polls, obvious as the limitations of the method are, the evidence they supply is even more impressive. A very large majority of the American people—perhaps as many as three-quarters or four-fifths—were apparently willing, a little while ago, to answer Yes to the proposition that their country should undertake to establish the Four Freedoms of the President 'everywhere in the world'. A more searching question as to ways and means would doubtless have discouraged some of those who answered Yes so readily, but the heavy majority in support of the general proposition is proof at least of the extent of active interest.

These moreover are not the only evidences of the public interest nor are they indeed the most convincing. It is, after all, by the talk of individuals and by the activities of small groups that the attitudes of populations are really judged, and judgments of this character in America to-day correspond closely to the evidence of the papers and the polls. It would be misleading to present the American people as wholly given over to discussion of the problems of the post-war world. The American people, like your-selves, have other things to think of from one day to the next. But it would be even more misleading to suppose that the American interest in these matters is superficial or sporadic—the consequence of Henry Wallace's fine speech or Sumner Welles's convincing presentation or the moving words of Mr Winant. On the contrary, the public con-cern came first and the speeches followed. It was the profound and creative interest of the people which pro-duced these declarations and others like them: not the declarations which produced the public interest. This series of official statements was not planned. It was not pro-jected in advance either by the government or by those who spoke. I should doubt that Mr Wallace and Mr Winant and Mr Welles and Mr Perkins and Mr Acheson consulted each other or had any other knowledge of each other's plans than the knowledge the newspapers provided to them all. They spoke as they did because the things of which they spoke were in their hearts as well as in their minds. Which is another way of saying that they spoke as they did because the things of which they spoke were in the hearts also of their listeners. The speeches which shape opinion in a democratic country are never the novel and unexpected speeches which break new ground and present new ideas. They are the speeches for which the people have prepared—the speeches the people have made possible—the speeches, indeed, which the people, through the mouths of their leaders, have uttered to themselves.

What has truly happened to American opinion of the

war and of the world may be judged, I think, with considerable accuracy by the simple fact that these several speeches were delivered and received. I should not wish, however, to leave you with the impression that these speeches have been accepted with a unanimity of agreement in the United States. On the contrary, they have been attacked with passion by minorities in the press and in the country. But the attack itself bears testimony to the extent and meaning of the changes which are taking place, for those who make it are the remnants of the isolationist minority of seven months ago. Isolationism in America is dead, as all the polls agree. But old isolationists never really die: they merely dig their toes in in a new position. And the new position, whatever name is given it, is isolation still. Where the old isolationism opposed the country's determination to face the war, the new isolationism opposes the country's determination to face the peace. The drawing of the lines along that issue shows the issue for what it is.

Prior to the attack upon us at Pearl Harbor when the American people were beginning to say to themselves that America existed in the common world, and that anything that touched the rest touched her, American isolationism was geographical—a sort of geophysics in reverse. We were surrounded by great quantities of water: therefore we were immune to history. Now that Pearl Harbor and the Atlantic U-boats have exploded that geographical immunity, and now that the American people are beginning to say to each other that America is at war and that wars occur not on battlefields only but in men's lives, and must have consequences in men's lives, American isolationism has dropped geography and turned to military science. Where the isolationists argued once that the country need not face the choice of war or peace because the waters were too wide, they argue now that the country need not face the choice of peace or chaos because the battles are too hard. It is a military error, they tell us, if not indeed a moral fault, to discuss the purpose of a war you have not won. It is a military irrelevancy, if not an evidence of moral decay, to plan for the consequences of a war in which your armies still retreat and your cities still surrender and your ships still sink.

The isolationists, in other words, are still isolationist and their isolationism still has for object the insulation of their country—by which they mean, of course, the insulation of the status quo within their country—from the history of the time. Driven from a policy of isolationist peace they have taken refuge in a policy of isolationist war. If they must have war, they will have a war which shall alter nothing and accomplish nothing: a war which shall have neither social effects nor political implications: a purely military war: a military exercise in which the dead may be dead and the cities may be destroyed but the manœuvres shall otherwise be manœuvres only and shall have no meaning. They have appropriated the war as before they sought to appropriate the American continent when they insisted that with *them* America came first. Their newspapers have become the most chauvinistic, their speeches the most flamboyant, the country affords. They hate the enemy with a public hatred rarely surpassed in any vocabulary. But the war they support with so much noise and fury is not the war the world is fighting but a very different war. It is not the people's war to which the United Nations have committed themselves— the war fought, as the President has put it, by the massed, angered forces of common humanity—but another war, a soldier's war, a war of military purpose only, a war which they hope will end, as their original policy of peaceful isolation was intended to end, with all the rights and perquisites intact, and everything put back the way it was before.

The significance of all this lies, not in any possible effect the isolationist attack may have upon American opinion, but in the fact that the isolationist attack has taken place. Isolationism itself, whether geographical or military, is a bankrupt movement. Time and history—the forces it attempted to resist—have exposed its empty hand. The isolationist leaders have been driven into indirection and apologetics and the isolationist press has been forced back upon a mean-spirited and vindictive propaganda of personal vilification which destroys itself. But the fact that the isolationist leaders and the isolationist press have elected to reform their broken lines upon the front of preparation for the peace, is proof that they too see the weight and movement of the people's minds.

And as to that they are not wrong. The American people, like the people of this country, have recaptured the current of history and they propose to move with it: they do not mean to be denied. They are no longer willing merely to fight the fascists' war—to accept the war forced upon them by their enemies and to fight back in that war and eventually to win it. They propose with your help and the help of their friends in Russia and in China and in other countries to fight their own war—a free man's war having free man's purposes. They are no longer satisfied, in other words, to fight a war merely to prevent something—to prevent defeat at the hands of the Nazis and their allies. They are determined to fight a war to accomplish something and they propose to consider, and to consider very carefully, what it is they should accomplish—what kind of victory they and you and the rest, the free peoples of many countries, should conceive and so create. They are determined, briefly, to fight a war which shall have consequences rather than a war insulated from consequences, and they wish to consider with each other and with you and with the rest what consequences are desirable and are to be obtained. They believe—they believe quite literally—that this is a people's war and not a soldier's war alone, for they see that it is a war in which the soldiers are the people and the people are the soldiers; and they have very little patience with those who speak of it, or think of it, solely in terms of manœuvre and weapons and campaigns, vital as these things are.

The truth is—and it is a truth we shall do well to recognize—that there is a stirring in our world: a gathering of human power—of the power of humanity: a forward thrusting and overflowing of human hope and human will which must be given channel or it will dig a channel for itself. The truth is that the people have come to recognize in the mirror of this dreadful war that they *are* the people and that the light is theirs. They have not talked to each other back and forth across the boundaries yet, but they can hear each other talking: they know that there is someone there—someone who can hear and speak and is the people also. There is a new sense of the people in the world—a sense which became palpable in the magnificent and yet heart-breaking and yet inexpressibly noble resistance of the people of London and the English towns; a sense which becomes from day to day more explicit as the people of Russia, under arms, fight inch by inch across their never-to-be-conquered country; a sense which the millions dead in China have made tragic and remembered.

The people know they did not make this war. They know it was not of their choosing: that it was forced upon them: that they undertook to fight not for some purpose of their own but in order to defend: to survive: to go on living. They were troubled for a time by the feeling that this war was not theirs—that it was a thing done *to* them and not *by* them. They were troubled too by the propaganda of their enemies which told them that they had no cause, that they were fighting for nothing, that the real cause was the cause of the Nazis and the fascists who had had the will to make the war and to attack—who knew what they wanted and how to secure what they wanted. The people were ashamed that it was necessary for them to fight a defensive war, to fight only to survive, and they were puzzled by the propaganda, but they knew also that it was propaganda and that it was not true.

They knew always, whether their leaders were willing to say it for them or not, that they had a cause—that they had indeed the one cause for which a war could possibly be fought and won. The name of that cause—the words for that cause—they could not immediately find. They turned back to the old words—to Lincoln talking of the people—to Lincoln addressing the Congress in the blackest year of the Civil War and telling his countrymen they would nobly save or meanly lose the last best hope of earth. They turned back to the old words and the old words came alive in their mouths and found new meaning. But even the greatest words can serve the course of history only once. There was something new now in the world, something forward in time, and the people felt it. They recognized it in each other's faces, in each other's courage, in the newspaper accounts of the resistance of the people elsewhere, in the radio stories from the many fronts. They knew that the President was right when he told them that the militarists of Rome and Tokyo and Berlin had begun this war, but that they would end it—that the people would end it. They propose to end it and to end it, not by defeating the purpose of the enemies of the people only, but by realizing a purpose of their own—a clear and forming purpose—a purpose to live like men, to live with dignity and in freedom, and like men.

It is this that has happened in the past few weeks. It is

a small thing perhaps—the welling up in the words of their leaders of the people's purpose—of the people's will. It is a small thing, but it will have consequences and it will not be denied. The free peoples, by their actions, will create the hope and meaning of their time and they will speak of it. They will speak of it now: not later. They will speak of it as they fight this war, and as a means to fight this war. For they know now that when they have found the words in which their purpose can be stated they will have found as well the weapon by which the war will have been won.

Lightning Source UK Ltd.
Milton Keynes UK
UKHW010623040820
367667UK00001B/90